Glass

C O N C E P T   S C I E N C E

Written by Colin Walker

Before sheets of glass were made,
windows were just holes in walls
that let the light in.

Castles, churches, and houses were often cold. As well as light, windows also let in the rain and wind.

The Egyptians and the Romans made glass to make beautiful vases and bottles.

Much later, colored glass was used for church windows. In time, small panes of glass were made for the windows in rich people's houses.

Skilled craftspeople used to shape
glass by blowing through long tubes.
They made ornaments, containers,
bottles, and small panes of glass.
Then, new ways of making glass
were discovered.

Today, special sand is heated up until it melts into glass. Usually, some limestone and soda are added, and the liquid goes through rollers to make sheets. Because glass can now be made in factories, everyone can have glass windows.

Because it is a liquid when it is hot, glass can be used in many ways.

It can be poured into many shapes, to make fish bowls, perfume bottles, round marbles, magnifying glasses, or flat sheets.

Very thin glass is used to make light bulbs. Thick, strong glass can be made into glass bricks for new buildings.

Glass can be made stronger if it is poured over plastic or wire.

8

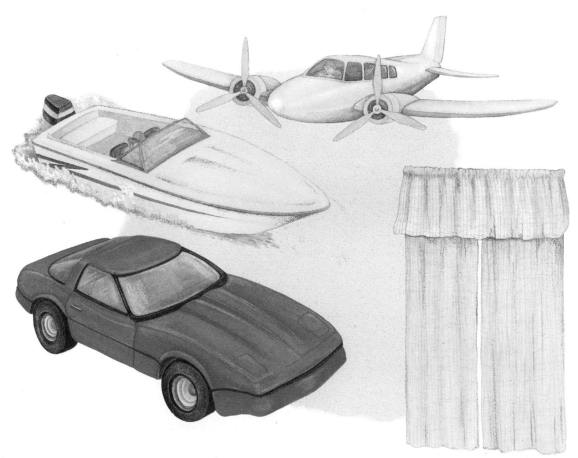

Very thin threads of glass can be
woven together to make fiberglass.
Fiberglass is used to make
parts of boats, airplanes, cars,
and even furniture and curtains.

Glass can be made in different colors. When gold is added to molten glass, it turns red. If cobalt is added to molten glass, it turns blue.

Glass does not rot or wear out easily.
It takes thousands of years for glass
to wear away into sand again.

In some museums, we can see glass
ornaments made over 5000 years ago.

Glass does not conduct electricity, so it is often used as an insulator on power poles.

It does not heat up easily, but it lets the sun's heat flow through it.

Glass is a bad conductor of heat and electricity.

Glass is an easy material to use because it keeps the shape it is made in, but it is brittle and breaks easily.

Then, glass can be dangerous!

QUIZ

What kind of glass are boats sometimes made of?

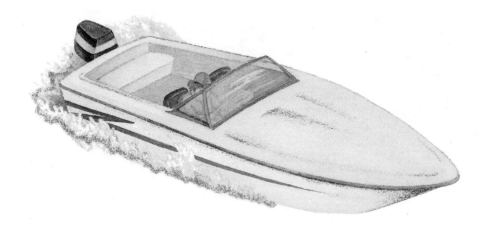

How can glass be made stronger?

Can curtains be made of glass?

Why is glass used to make insulators on power poles?

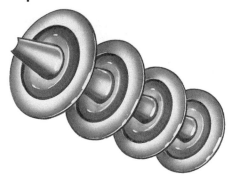

What is molten glass?

Try these activities:

1. Look at home for items made of glass. How is each one used? List each item under one of these categories: DECORATIVE, COOKING, BUILDING, or CONTAINER. Compare your chart with other students' charts. See if you listed similar items under the same category.

Decorative	Cooking	Building	Container
vase	measuring cup	windows	peanut butter jar

2. With other students, collect objects made of glass. Arrange them in order of the thickness of the glass. Do you see any connection between thickness and how the glass is used?